Ernie The Cat And The Mysterious Tail

By Tim Hamilton

First published in Great Britain in 2025 by TEP publishing

The Empire Publishers publishing
131 Finsbury Pavement, London EC2A 1NT

https://www.theempirepublishers.co.uk/

Our books may be purchased in bulk for promotional, educational, or business use.

Please contact The Empire Publishers at +44 20 4579 8116, or by email at
support@theempirepublishers.co.uk

First Edition August 2025

ISBN
PAPERBACK: 978-1-968326-68-5
HARDCOVER: 978-1-968326-69-2

Acknowledgment

The person who has been by my side ever since I started this project is my wife, Nathalie. She has always believed in me.

Dedication

I would like to dedicate this book to my granddaughter Sienna Clare and my grandson George Timothy.

About the Author

When I was a child in the 1960s, I found reading and writing very difficult. My lovely primary school in Totteridge did all they could to help me, but secondary school in the 1970s was much tougher. I didn't do well in exams and ended up in classes where not much was expected of us.

In the 1980s, I started a gardening business, which has now lasted over 40 years. I've always worked hard, perhaps too hard at times!

Then, in August 2023, during a little trip to Brighton, I picked up a children's watercolour set—and that small moment changed everything. I started painting and haven't stopped since

Painting isn't easy for me. I'm colour blind, so choosing the right colours can be tricky. I also live with Parkinson's, which means my hands tremble—imagine trying to draw while riding in a bumpy car! But even with these challenges, I keep going. Every time a picture appears on the page, it feels like magic.

I hope this story shows that no matter what challenges you face, creativity and joy can find you—often when you least expect it.

Meet Ernie the Cat!

Ernie is no ordinary cat, he's a curious, quirky little fellow with a personality of his own. His favourite hobbies include taking long, luxurious naps in the sun, being delightfully picky about his meals (only the fanciest treats will do!), and surprising everyone with his favourite game, hide and pounce!

When he's not sneaking around corners or dozing off on cozy cushions, you'll find Ernie completely captivated by the television. He loves watching all the colours and shapes dance across the screen, it's his own kind of movie night!

Ernie may be fussy, sleepy, and full of surprises, but that's exactly what makes him so lovable. Get ready to follow his everyday adventures and discover the world through his playful paws!

Ernie is Lucy's cat, whom she loves and plays with every day. He has the softest fur and the loudest purr you can imagine; his coat is black like the midnight sky. Every day, Lucy would give him a cuddle and decide what colour his bow tie would be; he had so many, but her favourite was a red tartan one.

Lucy is seven years old, with dark brown eyes that sparkle like polished chestnuts and olive skin that glows in the sun. Her long, curly brown hair bounces just past her shoulders as she sings her heart out—often to Ernie. She liked to think of it as their little concert time, though Ernie usually just blinked slowly, a bit confused, as if trying to figure out what language she was singing in.

Lucy also had two grey mice that she kept in a cage at the bottom of her bed. Her mum had bought them as a special treat for doing so well at school. She figured Ernie wouldn't mind—and who knows, maybe they could all play together? Ernie didn't really have an opinion about the mice, as they always seemed to be asleep or tucked up in their paper nest. As far as he was concerned, if it didn't purr, nap, or bring him snacks, it wasn't worth too much effort!

There were four things in Ernie's life that he did have an opinion on. Boy, did he love sleeping! This was his favourite pastime; he could do it all day if he was allowed. Next came eating—though he could be a bit fussy—being Lucy's pet, and, of course, going out with his mate Oscar at night.

Oscar is a grey cat that lives next door but always seems to be in Ernie's garden. Ernie thought Oscar was a mean cat when he first met him, but he wasn't mean at all. In fact, he was as soft as Ernie's fur coat.

Oscar had had a bit of a rough start to life, not finding a forever home until he was a bit older. But now, he thought of himself as Ernie's best friend—and perhaps even a bit of a singer. Every evening, Oscar greeted Ernie with a cheerful 'meow,' a flick of his tail, and sometimes a little musical number that he believed was very impressive. Whether Ernie agreed was another story entirely.

One night, when Ernie was fast asleep in his usual place at night-time on the floor next to Lucy's bed, he was snoring as usual, but today more loudly than normal. So loud that nobody heard Oscar sneak into the house, tiptoe up the stairs, and sit by Lucy's bedroom door.

Ernie had told Oscar all about the little mice that Lucy's mum had given her, so he thought he would come and see them for himself. Oscar felt really bad sneaking around, but he did want to see the mice. He made his way over to the cage door and peered inside. He couldn't quite see them, so he pressed harder against the door until there was a small noise, and the cage door swung open. He looked closer, and now he could see that there were a couple of tails and some ears poking out of some shredded paper and what sounded like... snoring.

Ernie woke up early. He liked to go and see the mice if they were up; they didn't seem to mind him when he got near the cage. But this morning, the mice were gone, and the cage door was wide open. Ernie had to find the mice before anything bad could happen to them because he didn't want to see Lucy upset.

First, he looked under the bed—lots of toys and dust, no mice. He clambered into the wardrobe—lots of shoes and more toys but no mice. Next was the toy box, which was quite tall. Still no mice and not that many toys!

They were definitely not in the bedroom; maybe they were in the bathroom? There weren't many places to hide in there, so he looked in the bath—nothing! In the laundry basket—nothing! He even looked in the cupboard under the sink. He was so busy looking for the mice that he hadn't noticed the mess he was making. His tail swished this way and that and had knocked over shower gel bottles, toilet rolls, and even the toothpaste onto the floor.

When he finally realised the mice were not in the cupboard, the toilet roll had unravelled, shower gel had leaked all over the floor, and then Ernie trod on the toothpaste, and it squirted like a fountain, adding to the mess that was already there.

Ernie sat at the top of the stairs. This was not going at all well, he thought. He yawned—such a big yawn—then he started to think about his nice warm basket in the room next door to the kitchen.

Ernie's normal day would be to wake up and trot downstairs, eat some breakfast, then go to his basket and fall asleep. Ernie knew that he had to find the mice and somehow get them back into their cage before Lucy woke up.

He ran down the stairs and stopped to look into the living room. It was a disaster; the mice had chewed holes in the new yellow sofa. There was yellow fabric and white cushion stuffing in a big pile in the middle of the room. Oh no, this was terrible.

Just as he was about to investigate the living room a bit more, he heard a noise coming from the kitchen—a plate smashed on the floor.

Lucy had accidentally left the fridge slightly open before she had gone to bed, and now the mice were in it. They had a nibble of something that looked like cheese, but it didn't taste of anything. Then, at the back of the fridge, there was a box that had a certain smell to it. Between the two of them, they had pushed and pushed until it fell out of the fridge and had broken open.

Oh my word, what a mess the mice had made! Milk was spilled everywhere, smashed eggs littered the floor, and broken plate fragments made it dangerous to walk near the fridge door. In the middle of all this chaos was a broken box with a big lump of cheese in it.

Ernie tiptoed around the broken bits of plate and licked up some of the milk. He didn't like the smell of the cheese, but he couldn't help himself from looking inside the fridge to see if there was anything he could eat. It was then he noticed little footprints. He looked in the direction of where they were heading. Ernie smiled; he knew exactly where they were going, so he trotted off to find them.

And there they were, cosy and safe in his basket.

Ernie snuggled in with them to make them feel safe, soon all three were fast asleep and snoring.

The End!

Get ready for more mischief and mystery in "Ernie the cat
no I won't eat that"

Keep an eye out, you never know what Ernie will
get up to next!

Follow Ernie & Oscar's adventures on Instagram:
@thebaldheadedgardener
@erniethecatofficial and
@theparkyauthor